S·U·M·M·E·R · N·I·G·H·T·S

S·U·M·M·E·R · N·I·G·H·T·S

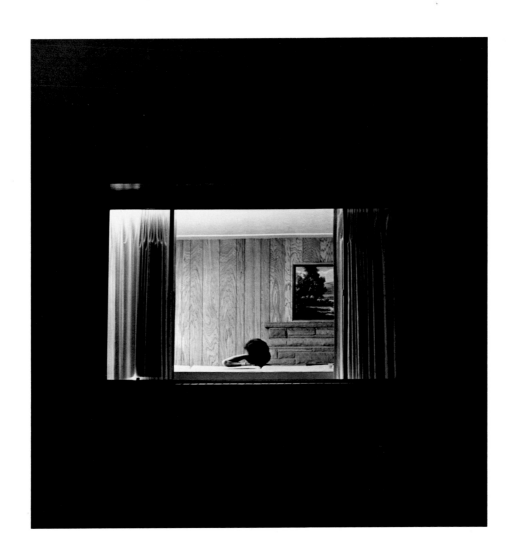

R·O·B·E·R·T · A·D·A·M·S

A NEW
IMAGES BOOK
APERTURE

I am grateful to Chris Sublett for his help during the taking of the pictures, and to Carole Kismaric for her support over many years. Without either of these friends the book would not have been completed.

Aperture, a division of Silver Mountain Foundation, Inc., publishes a periodical, books, and portfolios of fine photography to communicate with serious photographers and creative people everywhere. A complete catalog is available upon request. Address: Aperture, 20 E. 23rd Street, New York City, New York 10010.

For Carolyn, Michael, and James Dunn

Though I never properly photographed the evening
star, I saw it, and I repeat here Blake's poem to it as
my invocation:

.   .   .   .   .   .

Thou fair-hair'd angel of the evening,
Now, whilst the sun rests on the mountains, light
Thy bright torch of love; thy radiant crown
Put on, and smile upon our evening bed!
Smile on our loves, and, while thou drawest the
Blue curtains of the sky, scatter thy silver dew
On every flower that shuts its sweet eyes
In timely sleep. Let thy west wind sleep on
The lake; speak silence with thy glimmering eyes,
And wash the dusk with silver. Soon, full soon,
Dost thou withdraw; then the wolf rages wide,
And the lion glares thro' the dun forest:
The fleeces of our flocks are cover'd with
Thy sacred dew; protect them with thine influence.

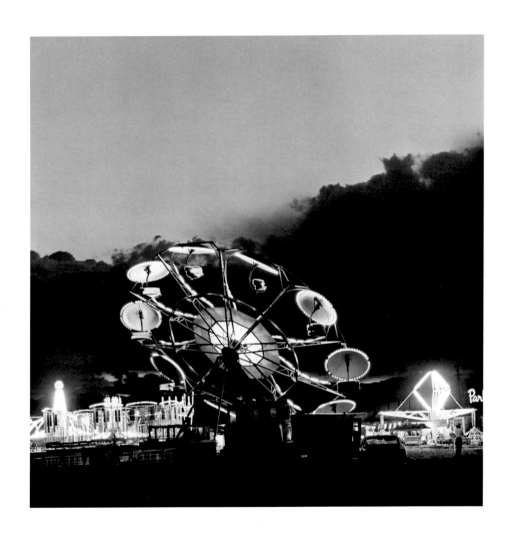

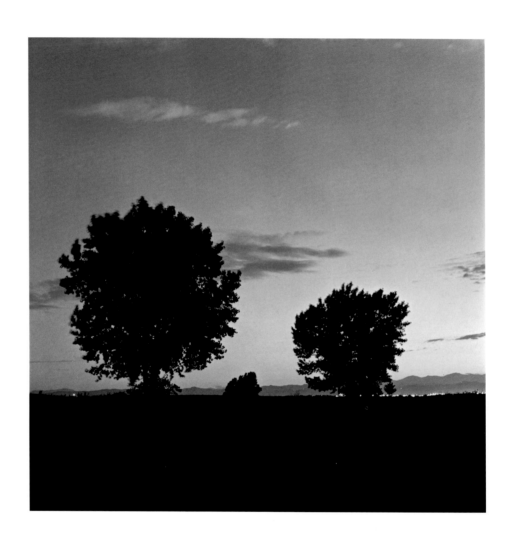

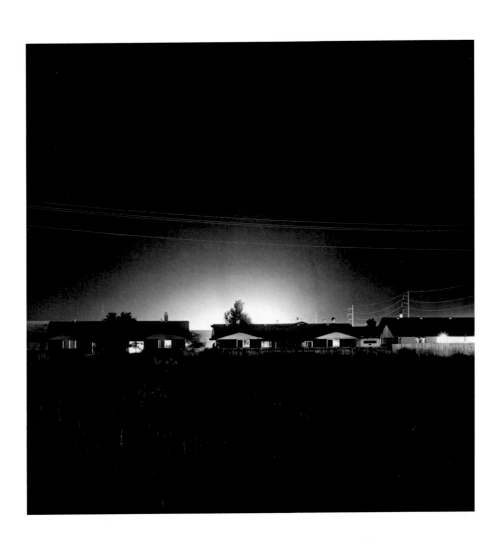

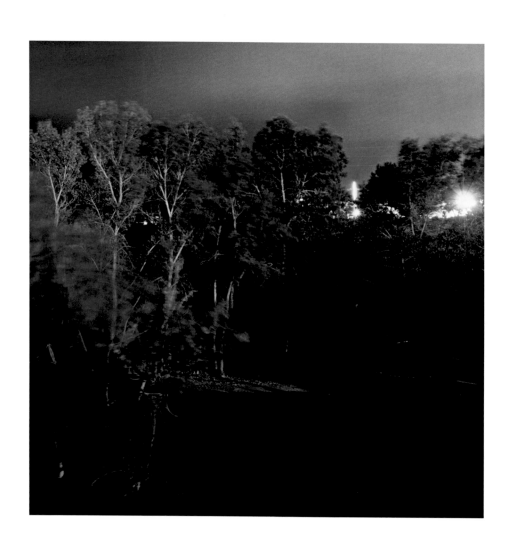

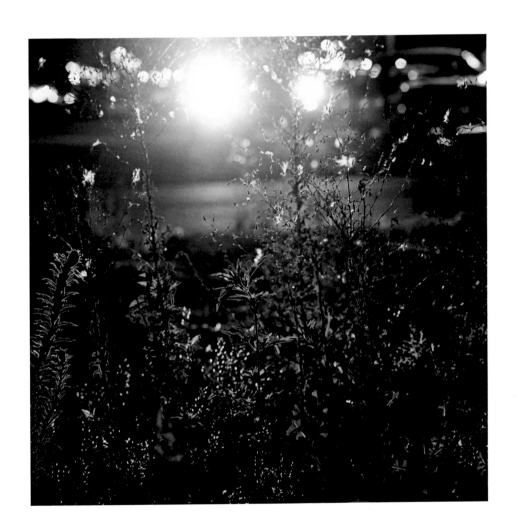

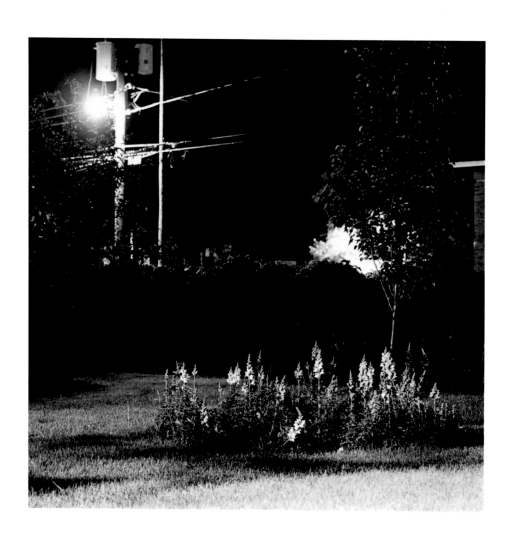

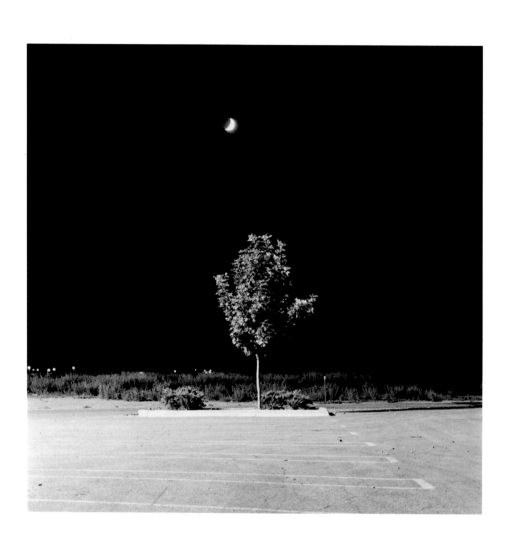

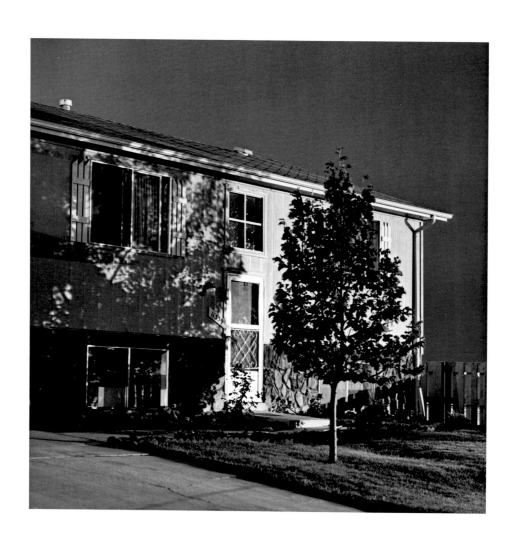

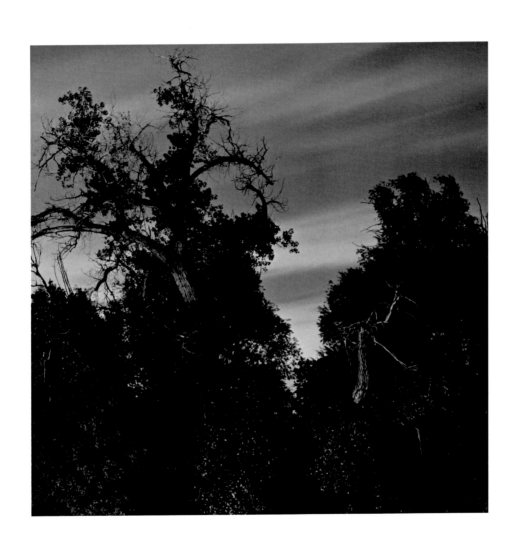

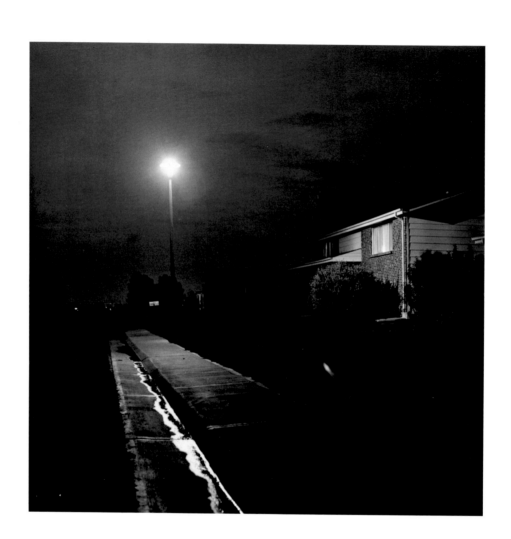

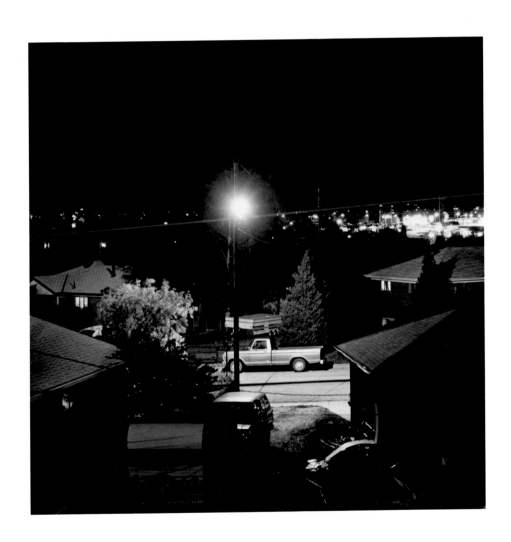

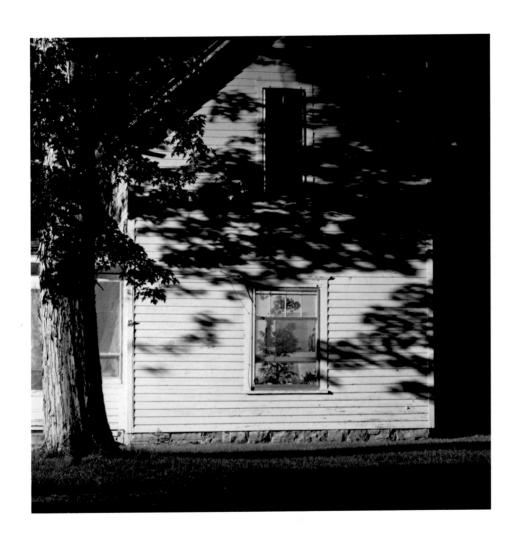

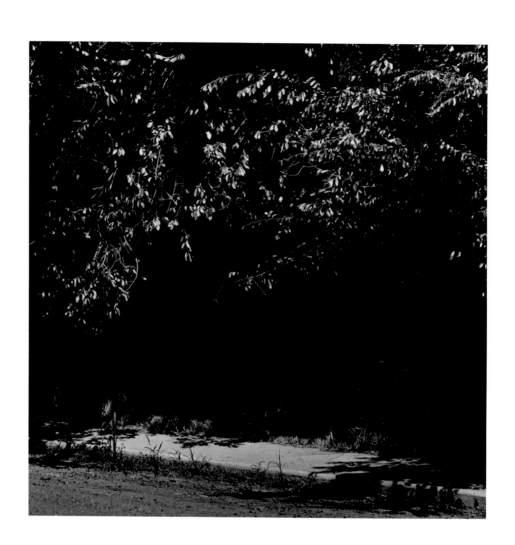

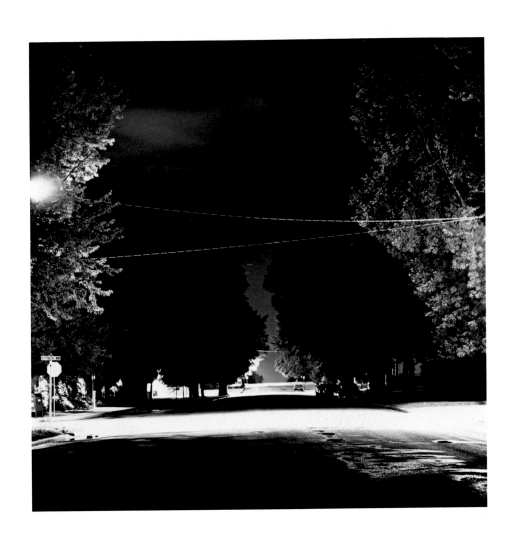

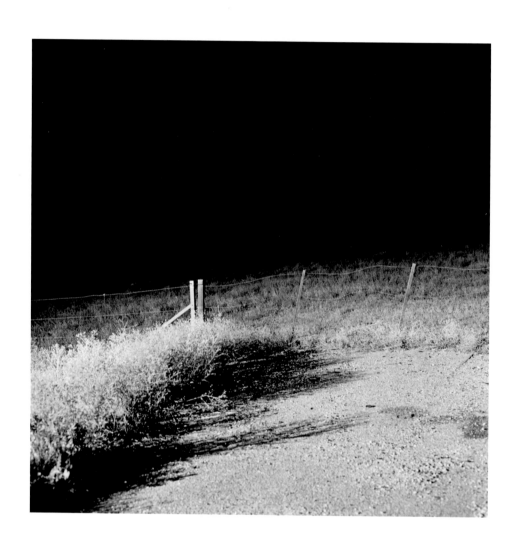

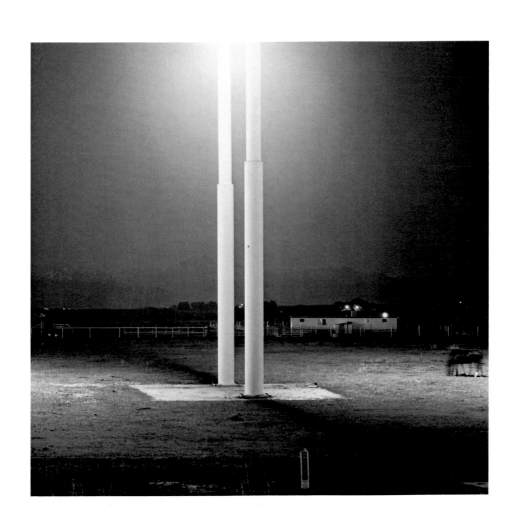

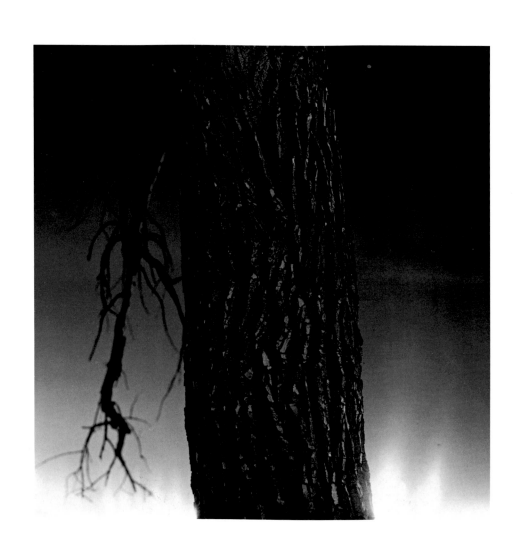

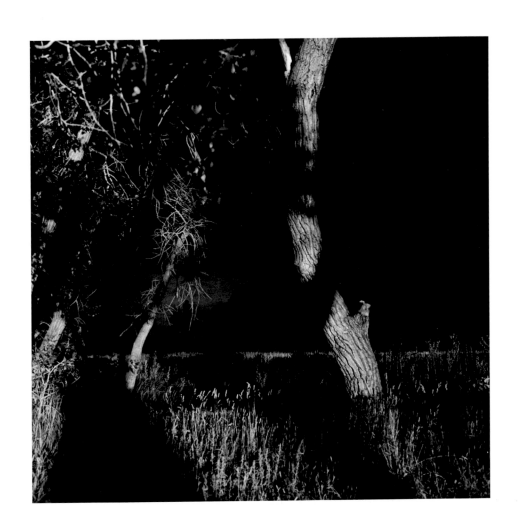

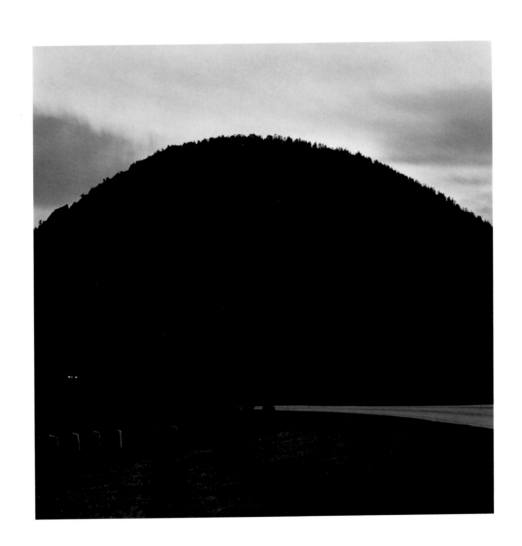

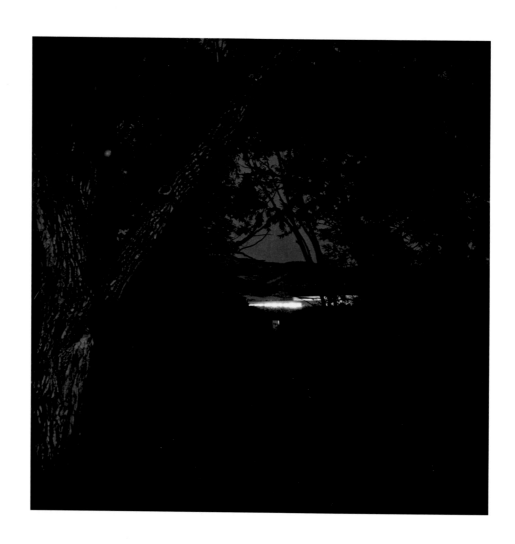

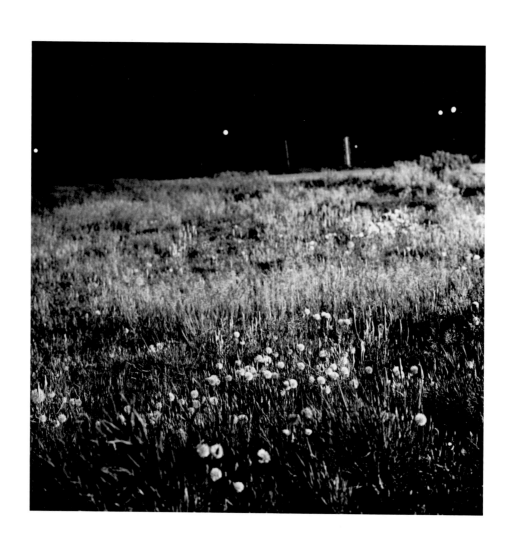

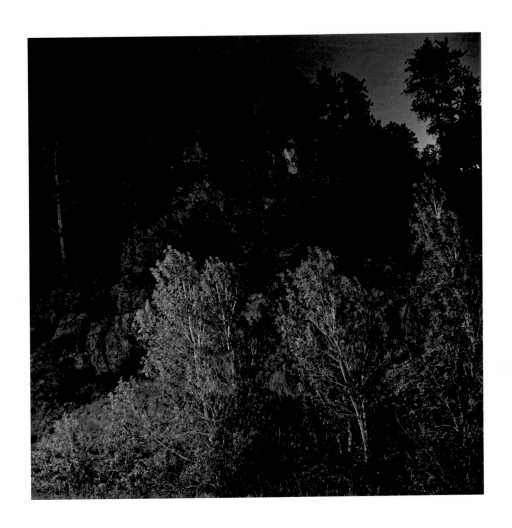

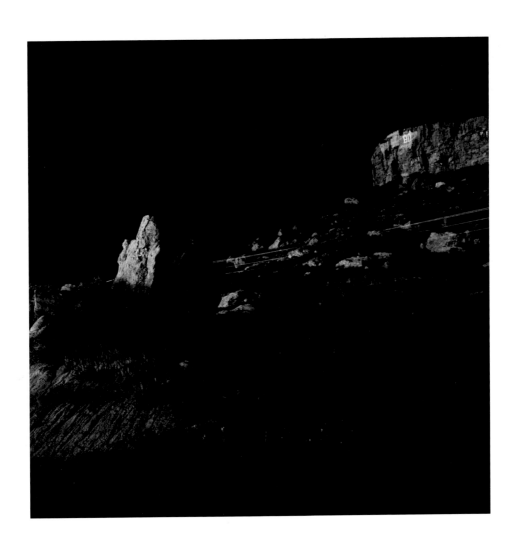